NATURAL RECORD BREAKERS

Jillian Powell

Heinemann is an imprint of Pearson Education Limited,
a company incorporated in England and Wales, having
its registered office at Edinburgh Gate, Harlow, Essex,
CM20 2JE. Registered company number: 872828

Heinemann is a registered trademark of Pearson Education Limited

OXFORD MELBOURNE AUCKLAND
JOHANNESBURG BLANTYRE GABORONE
IBADAN PORTSMOUTH (NH) USA CHICAGO

First published 1998

14

18

British Library Cataloguing in Publication Data
A catalogue record for this book is available from the British Library.

ISBN 978 0 435 09665 6   *Natural Record Breakers* single copy

ISBN 978 0 435 09666 3   *Natural Record Breakers* 6 copy pack

Photos: Ken Fisher / Tony Stone Images, page 5. Doug Scott / Chris Bonnington Library,
page 7. Georges Lopez / Still Pictures, page 8. Jorgen Schytte / Still Pictures, page 11.
Nick Haslam / Hutchinson Library, page 13. Kim Westerskov / Tony Stone Images, page
14. Tim Thompson / Tony Stone Images, page 17. Chris Sattlberger / Panos Pictures,
page 19. B. Regent / Hutchinson Library, page 21.

Illustrations: Steve Weston / Linden Artists, pages 4, 5, 7, 14, 20 and 22. The Maltings
Partnership, page 6. R.M. Lindsay, pages 9, 10 and 15. Julian Baker, pages 12 and 18.
Janos Marffy (Kathy Jakeman Illustration), page 16.

Thanks: Many thanks to Dr. Simon Carr of Oxford Brookes University for advising on the
manuscript, and to Helen Lantsbury of Oxford Brookes University for additional help

Designed by M2
Printed and bound in China (CTPS/18)

Contents

Introduction

This book looks at natural record breakers around the world, from the highest mountain to the deepest ocean. It describes the way they were formed and how big they are. It also looks at some of the plants and animals that live on and around them.

The HIGHEST waterfall

A waterfall forms when a river or stream falls over the edge of a rock or mountain. Water runs over hard rock, but if the rock is soft or **porous**, water can soak into it and **erode** it. This can leave a step of hard rock that water tumbles down.

How a waterfall forms

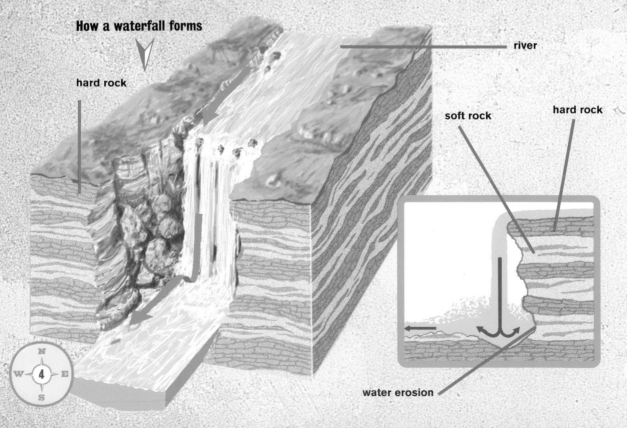

hard rock

river

soft rock

hard rock

water erosion

Angel Falls

The highest waterfall in the world is Angel Falls in Venezuela. The water drops for 979 metres. The waterfall was discovered in the 1930s by an American pilot called Jimmie Angel. He was flying over the mountains looking for gold when he found the falls.

Angel Falls is only visible from a boat or an aeroplane because it is in the middle of thick jungle.

Angel Falls is as high as three Eiffel Towers standing on top of each other.

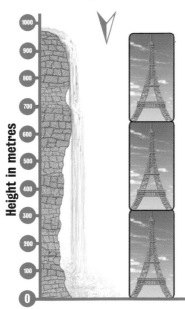

Angel Falls drop from Auyan Tepui in the Guiana highlands of Venezuela. 'Tepui' means 'mountain' in the local language. The falls are most spectacular during the rainy season, when they thunder down the cliff sending out clouds of spray.

The Devil's Mountain

Above the falls is a high sandstone **plateau**. Local people call it the Devil's Mountain because it is often covered with mist and cloud. Heavy rain falls there and feeds the Rio Churun river, which then falls over the edge of the plateau as Angel Falls.

Water animals

Giant otters live in the rivers near Angel Falls. They hunt for fish, eggs and birds. There are also animals called capybara. Capybara look like giant guinea-pigs, and grow to over a metre long. They are the biggest **rodents** in the world.

The HIGHEST mountain

The surface of the Earth is made up of slow-moving pieces, called plates, which fit together like a jigsaw. When two plates move towards each other, they push up the rock in between them to form mountains. These are called 'fold mountains'.

The plates move so slowly towards each other that the mountains can take millions of years to form. Mountains are found on land and under the sea.

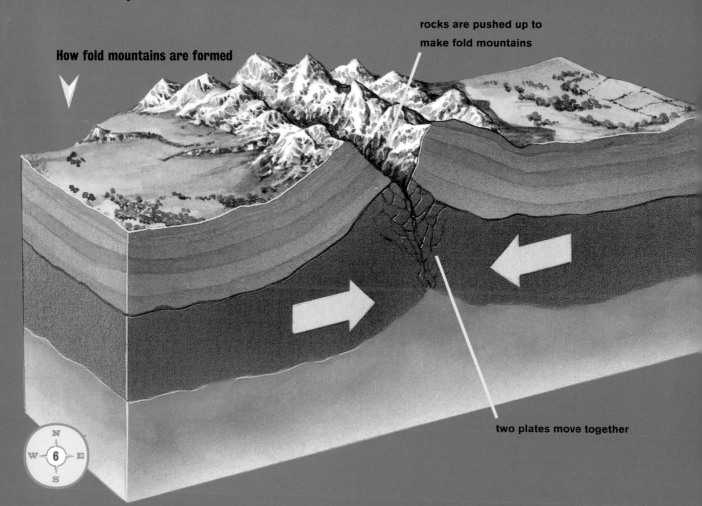

How fold mountains are formed

rocks are pushed up to make fold mountains

two plates move together

Mount Everest

The highest mountain is Mount Everest in the Himalayas. It stands 8848 metres high, on the border between Nepal and Tibet. As the plates that formed the Himalayas are still moving towards each other, the mountains continue to grow.

Mountain animals

Ibex and yak live on the mountainside. They are strong climbers. Their hoofs help them hold on to the rock and they have thick coats to keep them warm.

Mountain people

The Sherpa people live in valleys high in the Himalayan mountains. A Sherpa called Tenzing Norgay and Sir Edmund Hillary from New Zealand were the first people to reach the summit of Mount Everest. They climbed the mountain in 1953.

The Sherpa people tell stories about a monster called the yeti. They say it lives high in the Himalayas and is over two metres tall. Some people claim to have found giant footprints made by the yeti.

This chart shows the height of Everest in comparison with some other mountains.

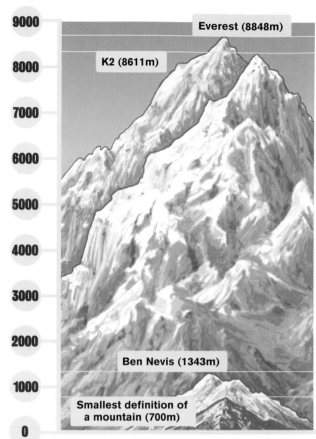

Height in metres

9000
8000
7000
6000
5000
4000
3000
2000
1000
0

Everest (8848m)

K2 (8611m)

Ben Nevis (1343m)

Smallest definition of a mountain (700m)

Himalaya means 'Home of Snows'. The air high up on the mountain is thin and does not contain much oxygen. Climbers wear oxygen masks to help them breathe.

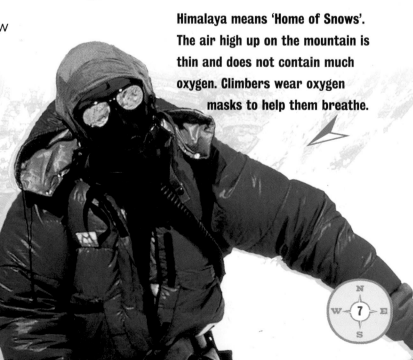

The BIGGEST desert

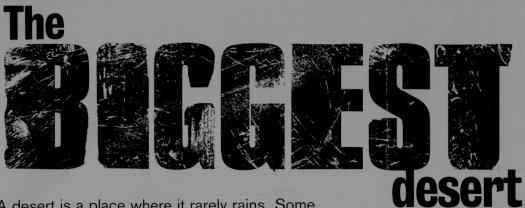

A desert is a place where it rarely rains. Some deserts are found in the middle of **continents**. Others lie in the shelter of high mountains. Most deserts are hot and dry, although some, such as the Gobi desert in China and Mongolia, are cold and dry.

The Sahara Desert

The biggest desert in the world is the Sahara in north Africa. It is almost as big as the United States of America and it reaches into eleven countries. It measures nearly 5000 kilometres from east to west, and 2000 kilometres from north to south.

The wind in the Sahara desert blows sand at rocks and erodes them, making them into strange shapes.

The desert landscape

The desert landscape is varied. Parts of the desert are flat; others are rocky and mountainous. There are also high sand dunes which are formed when strong winds blow across the desert.

Desert plants

Desert plants have to live and grow with very little rain. Cactus plants store rainwater in their stems, which helps them to survive. Date palms have long roots that can reach water deep underground.

Desert animals

During the day, the desert gets very hot. At night, it can be almost freezing. Some desert animals, such as the fennec fox, stay in their burrows during the day. They only come out when it is cooler to hunt for food.

Camels survive in the desert because they can live for a long time without water. They store fat in their humps, which provides them with water and **energy**. They also have long eyelashes and nostrils that close to keep out the sand.

Most people who live in the Sahara are nomads. They have to move around to find water and grow food. The Tuareg people travel great distances on camels, motorbikes or trucks.

date palm tree

camels

Tuareg people

fennec fox

9

The
LONGEST
river

Rivers shape valleys and carry water to farmland. People use them for water, as waterways for boats and for **energy** to make electricity. Many animals and plants live in and near rivers, and some of the world's most important cities have been built on the banks of rivers.

The Nile

The longest river in the world is the Nile in Africa. It flows for 6670 kilometres, which is as far as from London to New York. The river begins as the White Nile in Central Africa. About halfway along its journey, it is joined by the Blue Nile from Ethiopia. Then it flows north across the desert. It forms a **delta** before it meets the Mediterranean Sea.

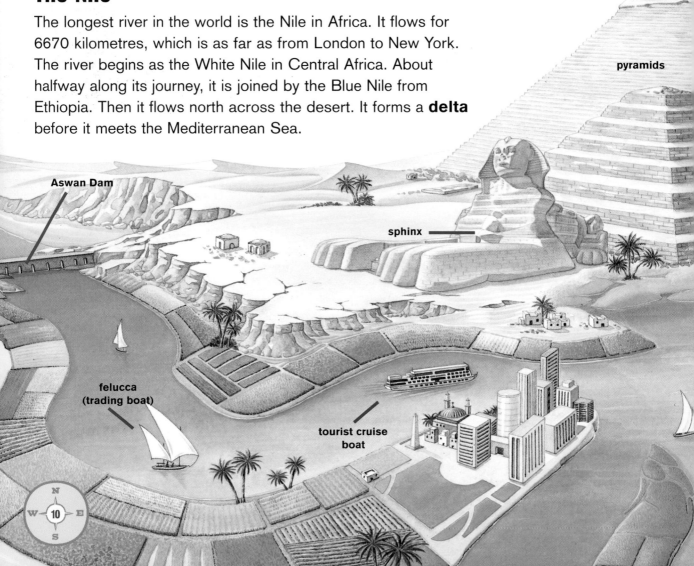

pyramids

Aswan Dam

sphinx

felucca
(trading boat)

tourist cruise
boat

 The Nile provides water for Cairo, the biggest city in Africa.

For about three thousand years, the Ancient Egyptians lived along the banks of the Nile. They grew crops in the rich black mud left by the river after it flooded each year. They built pyramids and many other huge buildings and statues.

The Aswan Dam stops the Nile from flooding each year and keeps water in Lake Nasser, which is the world's biggest man-made lake. Canals from the lake carry water to farmland. The water is also used to make electricity for Egypt's cities.

The source of the Nile

Explorers tried for many years to find the source of the Nile. In 1875 Henry Morton Stanley discovered that the source was the Ripon Falls above Lake Victoria in Burundi, Central Africa.

Nile animals and birds

Many animals, including crocodiles and hippopotamuses, live in the warm waters of the Nile. Birds such as pink flamingoes and African kingfishers feed on the fish that live in the river.

The BIGGEST cave

Caves are formed by rainwater creeping into cracks in rock. Acid in the rainwater **erodes** the stone and makes holes and tunnels underground. Most caves form in limestone. They can take thousands of years to form.

How caves are formed in limestone rock

cracks in rocks

cave

underground river

The Sarawak Chamber

The world's biggest cave chamber is the Sarawak Chamber in Borneo. It was discovered in 1980. It is one of many caves at the foot of Mount Api. The cave is 700 metres long and up to 120 metres high. It is big enough to hold twenty-three football pitches.

 Inside the Sarawak Chamber

Inside the cave

Inside the cave it is very dark, damp and cold. On the cave floor are huge rocks. Some are as big as houses. Water drips down from the cave roof and onto the floor. As it drips, a mineral called calcium carbonate turns hard in the cold air, forming **stalactites** and **stalagmites**.

Cave dwellers

The cave provides a home for bats, birds and insects. Bats hang from the cave roof during the day and hunt for food at night. Swiftlets make their nests in the caves. Spiders, scorpions and snakes live on the cave floor.

The area around Mount Api is a National Park and many of the caves are open to the public.

The DEEPEST ocean

Oceans and seas cover over two thirds of the Earth. The biggest and deepest ocean of all is the Pacific.

The Pacific Ocean

The Pacific covers almost a third of the Earth. It contains more water than the Arctic, Indian and Atlantic oceans put together. The widest part, between Malaysia and Panama in Central America, reaches nearly halfway round the world.

The ocean floor

The deepest part of the Pacific Ocean is called the Marianas Trench. It is over eleven kilometres deep, and is the deepest point on the surface of the Earth. If you dropped a kilogram weight into the water, it would take an hour to reach the bottom of the trench.

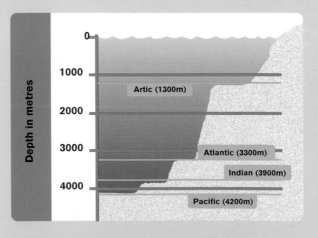

There are 25,000 islands in the Pacific, more than in the rest of the world's oceans added together.

This chart shows the depth of the Pacific in comparison with the world's other oceans.

Ocean explorers

The first people to explore the Pacific Ocean were Polynesian sailors over two thousand years ago. They sailed across the ocean, finding their way by the sun, the moon and the stars. Today, scientists use deep-sea craft to explore the ocean depths.

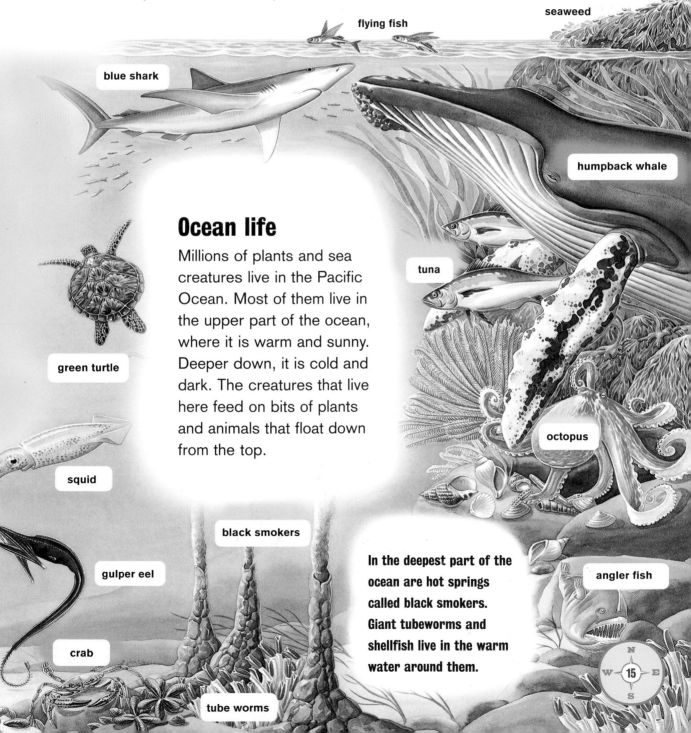

seaweed

flying fish

blue shark

humpback whale

Ocean life

Millions of plants and sea creatures live in the Pacific Ocean. Most of them live in the upper part of the ocean, where it is warm and sunny. Deeper down, it is cold and dark. The creatures that live here feed on bits of plants and animals that float down from the top.

tuna

octopus

green turtle

squid

black smokers

gulper eel

In the deepest part of the ocean are hot springs called black smokers. Giant tubeworms and shellfish live in the warm water around them.

angler fish

crab

tube worms

The LONGEST glacier

A glacier is a river made of ice. Glaciers form in high snowy mountains and in the coldest parts of the world, near the North and South **Poles**. Snow builds up on mountains, gradually getting deeper. Over tens of thousands of years, the bottom layer of snow turns to ice, and a glacier forms.

The weight of the ice causes glaciers to move. They flow faster if they are on a steep slope, and the ice is thick. They pick up rocks and stones on their way. These act like a giant pan scrubber, digging out a deep U-shaped valley.

Glaciers are found on every **continent** except Australia.

The end of a glacier is called its snout. When it reaches the snout, the ice begins to melt. If the glacier is running into the sea, pieces of ice can break off and form icebergs.

another glacier comes in from the side

glacier snout

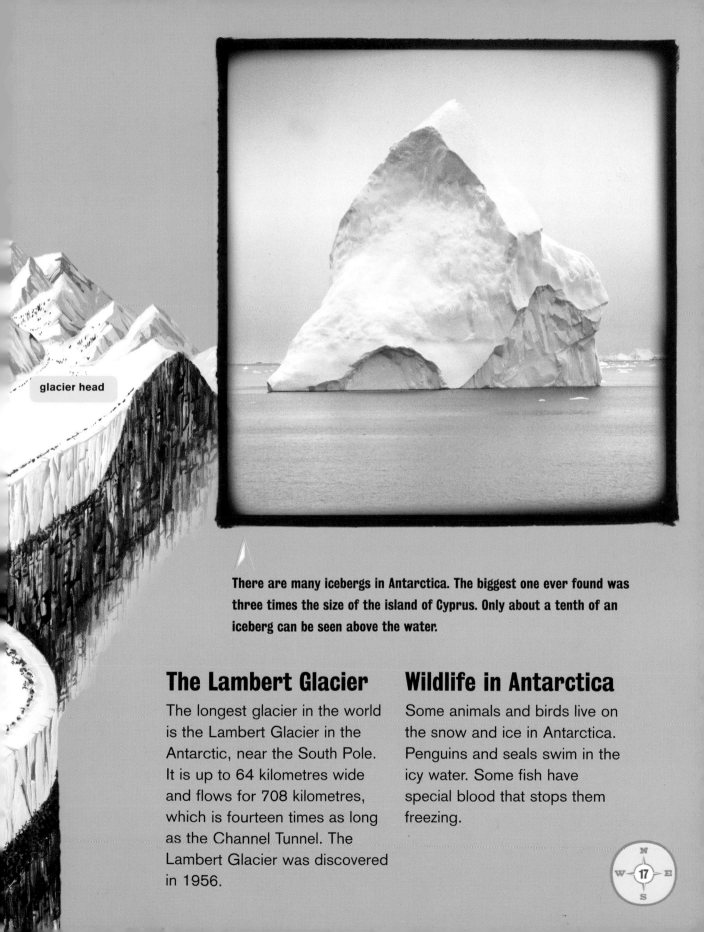

glacier head

There are many icebergs in Antarctica. The biggest one ever found was three times the size of the island of Cyprus. Only about a tenth of an iceberg can be seen above the water.

The Lambert Glacier

The longest glacier in the world is the Lambert Glacier in the Antarctic, near the South Pole. It is up to 64 kilometres wide and flows for 708 kilometres, which is fourteen times as long as the Channel Tunnel. The Lambert Glacier was discovered in 1956.

Wildlife in Antarctica

Some animals and birds live on the snow and ice in Antarctica. Penguins and seals swim in the icy water. Some fish have special blood that stops them freezing.

The BIGGEST
live volcano

A volcano forms through a hole in the Earth's **crust**. If the volcano is live, it may **erupt**, throwing hot molten rock called lava, gas and ash out of the top. There are about 850 live volcanoes in the world, and many more that are **dormant** or **extinct**. Most of the world's live volcanoes lie in a ring around the Pacific Ocean, called the Ring of Fire.

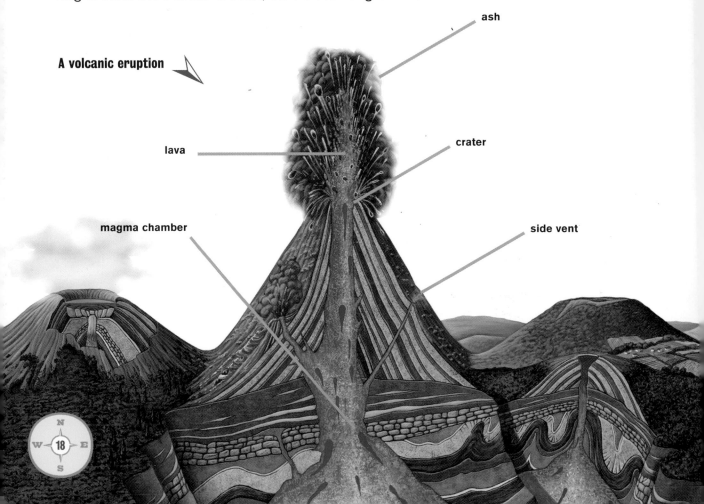

A volcanic eruption

ash

lava

crater

magma chamber

side vent

Mauna Loa

The biggest live volcano in the world is on the island of Hawaii. It is called Mauna Loa, which means Long Mountain. Mauna Loa is 9000 metres high. It is higher than Mount Everest, but over half of it lies under the sea.

Mauna Loa is one of two live volcanoes on Hawaii. One eruption lasted for over a year and a half.

Volcanic landscape

Around the volcano, hot springs called geysers and hot mud pools bubble up through cracks in the ground. Clouds of hot steam and gas escape. There is a strong smell like old eggs which comes from the gases underground.

Volcanic rock

Mauna Loa is made of a hard, dark rock called basalt. Basalt forms when lava pours out of the crater and side vents of a volcano. When it cools down, it becomes a layer of hard rock.

The BIGGEST gorge

A gorge is a very deep valley between steep walls of rock. It takes millions of years for a gorge to form. Gorges can be formed in two different ways. Sometimes the flowing water in a river gradually **erodes** the riverbed, so the banks become steep walls. In other cases, gorges are formed when the roof of a cave collapses, exposing an underground river.

How a gorge is formed

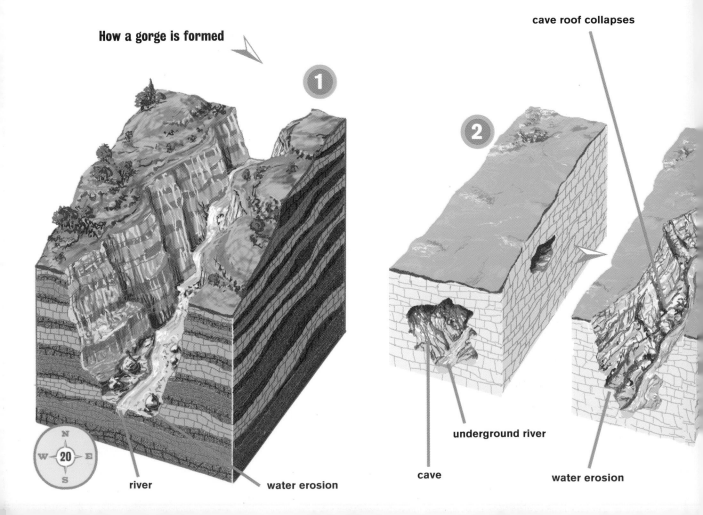

1

2

cave roof collapses

underground river

cave

river

water erosion

water erosion

20

The Grand Canyon

The Grand Canyon in Arizona, in the United States of America, is the biggest gorge in the world. It was formed about 60 million years ago, just after the age of the dinosaurs. Two rivers joined to make the Colorado River which wore away the riverbed to form the gorge.

The Grand Canyon is so deep it would take a whole day to walk from the rim down to the river and back again. It is 450 kilometres long, up to 29 kilometres wide and 1.6 kilometres deep.

The rock which makes up the gorge walls ranges from yellow to dark red in colour. The oldest rocks are in the deepest part of the gorge. They are made from the remains of old volcanoes.

The Colorado River runs from the Rocky Mountains to the Gulf of California.

Climate

The gorge is so deep that the **climate** at the top is different from the climate at the bottom. The coldest parts at the top can be covered in three metres of snow in winter. But deep down on the canyon floor, the land is hot, dry desert.

Plants and animals

Deer and squirrels live in the pine forests around the top of the gorge. Grey foxes and chipmunks live on the cool gorge walls. Cactus plants grow on the dry, desert land just above the river, where scorpions, snakes and lizards live.

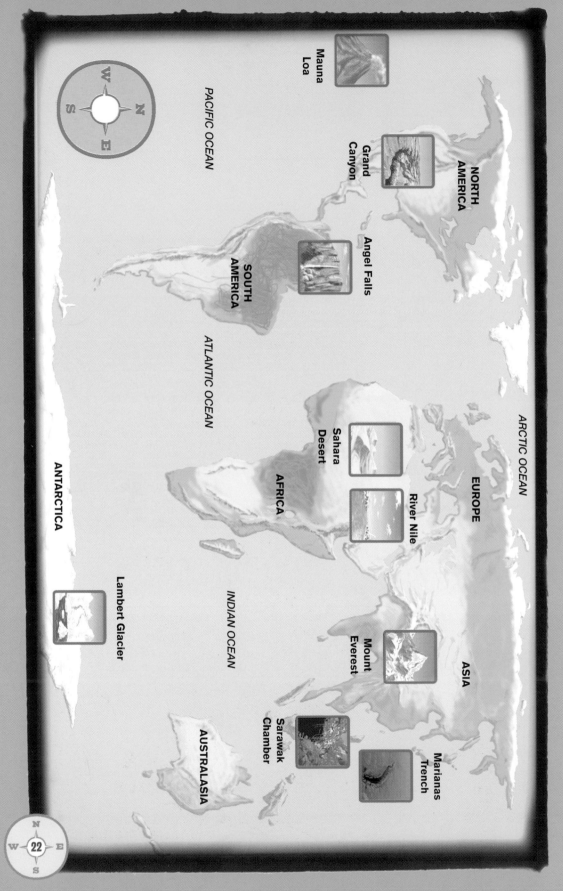

Mauna
Loa

PACIFIC OCEAN

Grand
Canyon

NORTH
AMERICA

Angel Falls

SOUTH
AMERICA

ATLANTIC OCEAN

ARCTIC OCEAN

Sahara
Desert

AFRICA

River Nile

EUROPE

ANTARCTICA

Lambert Glacier

INDIAN OCEAN

Mount
Everest

ASIA

Sarawak
Chamber

Marianas
Trench

AUSTRALASIA

N
W E
S

Glossary

climate
the kind of weather a place has

continent
one of the world's seven great land masses

crust
the surface of the Earth

delta
a triangle of land where a river fans out before it meets the sea

dormant
sleeping; not active

energy
the power to make things work or move

erode
to wear away

erupt
to pour out lava

extinct
dead; finished

nomad
a person who moves from place to place to find water and grow crops

plateau
a flat high area of land

pole
the north or south point at either end of the Earth

porous
containing holes that let water or air pass through

rodent
an animal with sharp teeth, such as a mouse, rat or squirrel

stalactite
a stone column made by water dripping from the ceiling of a cave

stalagmite
a stone column made by water dripping onto the floor of a cave

Index